STUDENT'S ACTIVITY BOOK for

Introduction to Jewish History

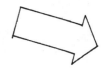

Abraham to the Sages

Malka Leah Avrami

Behrman House, Inc.

For the mishpacha

Published by Behrman House, Inc., 11 Edison Place,
Springfield, New Jersey 07081
ISBN: 0-87441-363-X

Illustrations by Richard Rosenblum
Cover/Book design by Marsha Picker

Contents

Fill The Box*

Put the first letter of each object in the box below it.

Write the letters here:

_____

This word is a Jewish idea that changed the history of the world. What does the word mean?

_____

Picture Detective

The picture on page 10 in your textbook shows Abraham and Sarah beginning their journey to Canaan. In the background you can see a *ziggurat*, a Mesopotamian pyramid. Ziggurats were tall. The people thought their pagan god lived at the top of this high place. Could a *ziggurat* help explain the name by which Abraham referred to God—*El Elyon*? What do you think?

_____

_____

_____

_____

_____

_____

True or False*

Circle the letter under True or False.

		True	*False*
1.	Jewish history began with Adam and Eve.	L	C
2.	Abraham left Canaan and traveled to Mesopotamia.	X	A
3.	Pagans worshipped many gods.	N	R
4.	Abraham and Sarah did not worship the pagan gods.	A	P
5.	Abraham made a covenant, a special agreement with God.	A	P
6.	In return, God promised to make the Israelites a great nation.	N	O
7.	The words of the covenant appear in the Book of Genesis in the Bible.	I	F
8.	Abraham sacrificed his son Isaac.	C	T
9.	The term "promised land" comes from a song.	S	E
10.	Circumcision is a sign of the covenant.	S	B

Write the letters you circled in the spaces:

Abraham and Sarah traveled to the land of the

— — — — — — — — — —.

Design A Standard

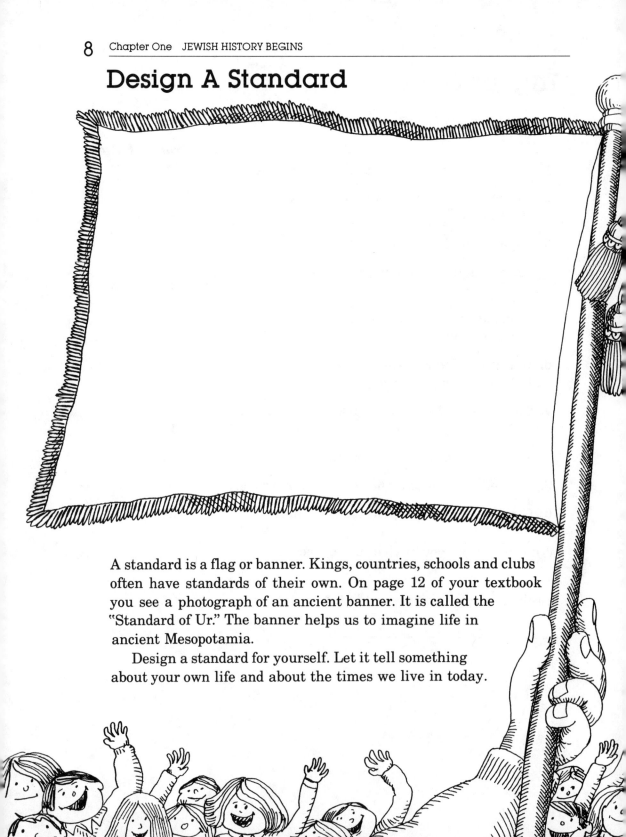

A standard is a flag or banner. Kings, countries, schools and clubs often have standards of their own. On page 12 of your textbook you see a photograph of an ancient banner. It is called the "Standard of Ur." The banner helps us to imagine life in ancient Mesopotamia.

Design a standard for yourself. Let it tell something about your own life and about the times we live in today.

Map Study*

Look at the map on page 18 of your textbook. It shows the route Abraham took on his journey. Study the map and then fill in the blank spaces below.

Abraham started in __ __ __ __ __ __ __ __ __. He began in the city of __ __. He did not go directly from east to west. The desert lay in between and offered no stopping places. Instead, he went along the __ __ __ __ __ __ __ __ __ __ River to __ __ __ __ and __ __ __ __ __ and from there on to __ __ __ __ __ __.

List two places in Canaan where Abraham might have stopped.

_____   _____

Adding Up History*

Take the number of Jacob's sons   _____

Subtract the number of Jacob's wives   − _____

Add Moses' age when he went to ask Pharaoh
to let the Jewish people go   + _____

Subtract Aaron's age at that time   − _____

Add the chapter number in the Book of Exodus
that tells about the Burning Bush   + _____

The total is the number of plagues brought upon
Egypt   = _____

Find The Hidden Message*

Moses' brother, Aaron, and his sister, Miriam, were with him in the desert. We know that Aaron was the high priest. Miriam was a musician and a singer. This was the victory song she sang when the sea swallowed Pharaoh's army.

(S)ING   TO   THE   LORD

(F)OR   HE   HAS   TRIUMPHED GLORIOUSL(Y)

HORS(E) AND   DRIVER

HE HAS HURLED IN(T)O THE SE(A)!

Write the circled letters here:

◯ ◯ ◯ ◯ ◯ ◯

Unscramble the letters:
God brought the Israelites from danger to

— — — — — —

In what book of the Bible is Miriam's song found?

_____

Multiple Choice*

Circle the phrase that best completes the sentence.

1. Moses, adopted by an Egyptian princess, was

   a. an Egyptian boy   **b.** a Hebrew boy   **c.** a pagan boy

2. Moses had to flee from Egypt because he killed an Egyptian who was

   a. refusing to work   **b.** beating a Jew   **c.** mining ore

3. The name of Moses' wife was

   a. Miriam   **b.** Matzah   **c.** Zipporah

4. When Moses came to Mount Horeb he saw

   a. a burning bush   **b.** frogs   **c.** a ram in a tree

5. God sent Moses back to Egypt to

   a. buy food   **b.** free the Jewish slaves   **c.** climb the pyramids

6. The picture on page 16 of your textbook shows Egyptian slaves

   a. preserving food   **b.** worshipping idols   **c.** making bricks

7. Pharaoh freed the Jewish slaves after plague number

   a. nine   **b.** four   **c.** ten

8. Free at last, the Jewish slaves left Egypt and set out for

   a. Canaan   **b.** Mount Horeb   **c.** Jethro

9. The dough the Israelites took with them from Egypt became

   a. ḥallah   **b.** matzah   **c.** dollars

10. The departure of the Israelites from Egypt is celebrated on

    a. Shavuot   **b.** Ḥanukkah   **c.** Passover

Word Search*

Look across and down to find ten words that tell something about Israelites in the wilderness. When you find a word, circle it.
Write the words you find on the lines below.

```
A  F  O  R  T  Y  M  L  X  P  M
T  A  L  T  A  R  A  L  A  W  B
O  A  D  E  W  L  N  A  R  K  L
R  B  C  A  L  F  N  G  X  E  D
A  P  L  R  S  T  A  B  L  E  T
H  U  N  S  I  N  A  I  V  Y  L
```

_____   _____

_____   _____

_____   _____

_____   _____

_____   _____

Lost In The Wilderness

Can you find your way from Egypt to Canaan?

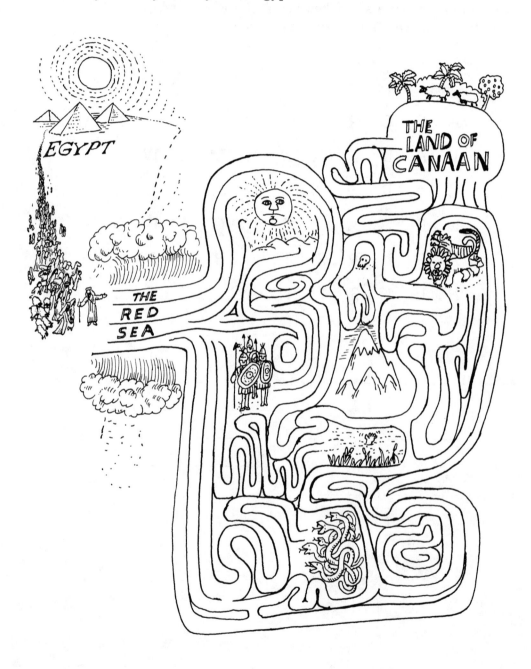

Word Puzzle*

What did the Israelites eat in the wilderness? To find out, fill in the words across. The answer is 1-down.

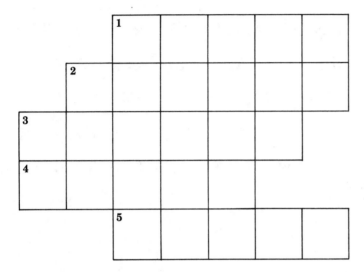

Across

1. Who was their leader?
2. What did they do in the wilderness?
3. Of what did they complain?
4. What did the special food they gathered taste like?
5. Who was Moses' brother?

Find The Hidden Word*

This is part of one of the Ten Commandments:

YOU SHALL NOT MAKE F(O)R YOURSELF
A S(C)ULPTURED IMAGE, OR ANY
LIKE(N)ESS OF WHA(T) IS IN THE
HEA(V)ENS ABOVE, OR O(N) THE EARTH
BELOW, OR IN THE W(A)TERS UNDER
THE (E)ARTH.

Write the circled letters here:

◯ ◯ ◯ ◯ ◯ ◯ ◯

Unscramble the letters:

God made a __ __ __ __ __ __ __ __ with the Jewish people.

Can you think of other words with the same meaning? (Look in a dictionary if you need help.)

_____   _____   _____

_____   _____   __

You Are There

The ancient rabbis said that whenever we say the *Shema* prayer, it is as if we are standing at the foot of Mount Sinai. Pretend that you are at Mount Sinai. Write about the events in your own words.

_____

_____

_____

_____

_____

_____

_____

_____

_____

_____

Ancient Warfare

These weapons were used in ancient battles. Label each one and write whether it was used by the Israelites or Canaanites.

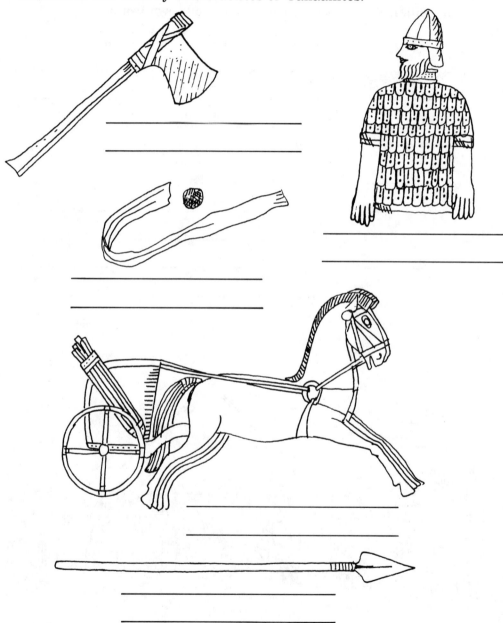

_____

_____

_____

_____

_____

_____

_____

_____

_____

_____

True or False*

Circle the letter under True or False.

		True	False
1.	Caleb led the Israelites into Canaan.	T	M
2.	The Israelites settled in the valleys.	E	I
3.	When Israelites fought they wore heavy armor and rode in chariots.	O	D
4.	The lands that the Israelites won in battle were in the hills.	I	P
5.	When Canaan was conquered, it was divided up among the twelve tribes.	A	R
6.	The Israelites fought the Canaanites in order to remove idol worship from the land.	N	S
7.	The land was promised to the Israelites by Menachem Begin.	B	I
8.	El was the name of a Canaanite hill.	C	T
9.	The judges were rulers and generals in Canaan.	E	F
10.	The Book of Joshua is in the Bible.	S	G

Write the letters you circled in the spaces:
The fierce camel-riding people defeated by Gideon were called the

— — — — — — — — —.

Map Study

The map on page 29 of your textbook shows how the land was divided among the twelve tribes of Israel. List the tribes that received lands north and south of Jerusalem.

*Tribes North
of Jerusalem*

*Tribes South
of Jerusalem*

_____   _____

_____   _____

_____   _____

_____

_____

_____

_____

_____

Atten–tion!!

You have read in your textbook that the judges were like generals. Gideon was a famous judge and a clever and strong leader. He led three hundred farmers in an attack, but the Midianites thought they were surrounded by a great army. How did Gideon surprise the Midianites?

_____

_____

_____

_____

_____

Fill The Box*

On page 22 of your textbook you see an artist's drawing of the Israelites carrying the Ark of the Covenant. On page 32, you see a photograph of a stone carving of an ark found in a 1st Century synagogue. On page 36 you see another drawing of the ark, as King David danced before it.

Put the first letter of each picture word in the box.

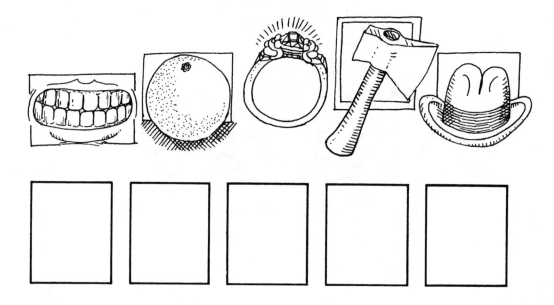

What do we keep in the ark today?

_____

Word Puzzle*

What city did David choose for his capital? To find out, fill in the words across. The answer in 1-down.

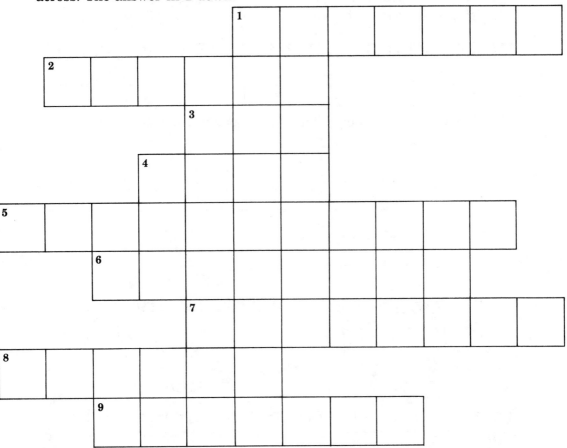

Across

1. With what animal part did Samson kill thousands of Philistines?
2. Who named the first king of Israel?
3. In what were the commandments kept?
4. Who was the first king of Israel?
5. Which enemy did David fight?
6. Who was David's best friend?
7. What did the Phoenicians give to the world?
8. What does the root of the word *Phoenician* mean in Greek?
9. Besides Hebrew, what language did the Israelites speak?

Unscramble The Idea*

You have read that the Phoenicians introduced the alphabet to the world. Unscramble the letters below to see the important idea the Jewish people gave to the world.

N E O   O D G   L U R S E   E V R O   L A L

___ ___ ___   ___ ___ ___   ___ ___ ___ ___ ___   ___ ___ ___ ___   ___ ___ ___

In what ways is this idea different from pagan beliefs?

_____

_____

_____

_____

_____

Multiple Choice*

Circle the phrase that best completes the sentence.

1. The Israelites wanted a king because they wanted to

   a. be like other nations   **b.** worship him   **c.** go to war

2. Samuel was opposed to the idea because

   a. only God should be king   **b.** everyone would want to be king
   c. there was no palace in the land

3. Samuel gave in to the people's wish and named _____ king.

   a. David   **b.** Saul   **c.** Jonathan

4. Because the king was in a bad mood his attendants brought David to play the _____ for him.

   a. piano   **b.** clarinet   **c.** harp

5. David was a good musician and also a good

   a. warrior   **b.** chef   **c.** carpenter

6. At first Saul liked David, but then he

   a. grew jealous of his popularity   **b.** sent David home   **c.** grew tired of David's songs

7. Saul's son Jonathan

   a. resented David   **b.** was David's best friend   **c.** didn't like the way David sang

8. Saul tried to kill David, and David

   a. was forced to flee   **b.** fought back   **c.** refused to leave

9. In the end, Saul and Jonathan were killed in a battle with

   a. Deborah   **b.** bandits   **c.** the Philistines

10. David became a great king and chose _____ to be his capital.

    a. Shiloh   **b.** Jerusalem   **c.** Tyre

Label the Ships*

You have read how Israel became rich under King Solomon's rule. Solomon built many ships and hired Phoenician sailors to bring cargoes to Israel.

On this map you see ships sailing to Solomon's land. Label each ship with the cargo it might be carrying.

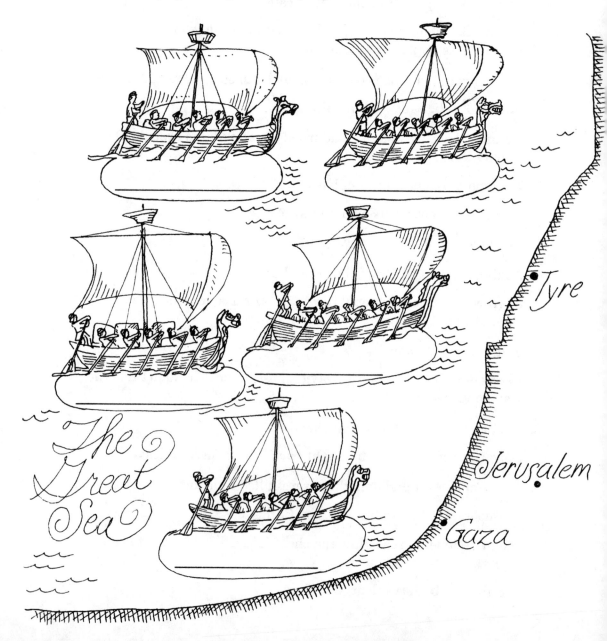

Find the Hidden Phrase*

DAVID APPOINTED A SCRIBE TO
            16   2

TAKE DOWN IN WRITING
     11   8

EVERYTHING THAT HAPPENED,
          12   9

AND A MAN TO ANNOUNCE NEW

LAWS TO THE PEOPLE. HE
5   13

APPOINTED TWO HIGH PRIESTS
1

IN JERUSALEM TO OFFER
        3   15

SACRIFICES TO THE LORD, AND
                      14

THEN APPOINTED GOVERNORS
     4   10

AND JUDGES FOR THE MANY
                      7

PARTS OF THE KINGDOM.
                  6

Write the numbered letters in the spaces to see what happened when David's son tried to become King.

___ ___ ___ ___ ___ ___ ___   ___ ___ ___   ___ ___ ___ ___ ___ ___
 1   2   3   4   5   6   7   8   9   10   11   12   13   14   15   16

Multiple Choice*

Circle the phrase that best completes the sentence.

1. The Temple in Jerusalem was built by

   a. David   **b.** Solomon   **c.** the Philistines

2. The main feature of the Temple was that it held

   a. the Ark of the Covenant   **b.** cedar pillars from Lebanon
   c. the Gezer calendar

3. When music was made part of the Temple service,

   _____ were among the many instruments that were played.

   a. xylophones   **b.** flutes   **c.** pianos

4. The Israelites went to the Temple in Jerusalem three times
   a year to

   a. offer sacrifices   **b.** hear the megillah   **c.** celebrate the
   olive crop

5. Jerusalem was also know as

   a. the City of David   **b.** the city of light   **c.** the birthplace of David

6. The Temple in Jerusalem was supported by cedar trees from

   a. Egypt   **b.** Queen Sheba's forests   **c.** Lebanon

7. The poets who wrote for Solomon's court created what is known as

   a. wisdom literature   **b.** commentaries   **c.** laws

8. Solomon is best known for his

   a. wardrobe   **b.** wisdom   **c.** many wives

9. The Gezer Calendar of the 10th century B.C.E.

   a. lists king's birthdays   **b.** lists ancient holidays
   c. tells farmers when to plant and when to harvest

My Own Calendar

The Gezer calendar outlines the farmer's year in ancient Israel about 3,000 years ago. You have seen a picture of the calendar in your textbook (page 43). Use the space below to create a calendar that outlines your year.

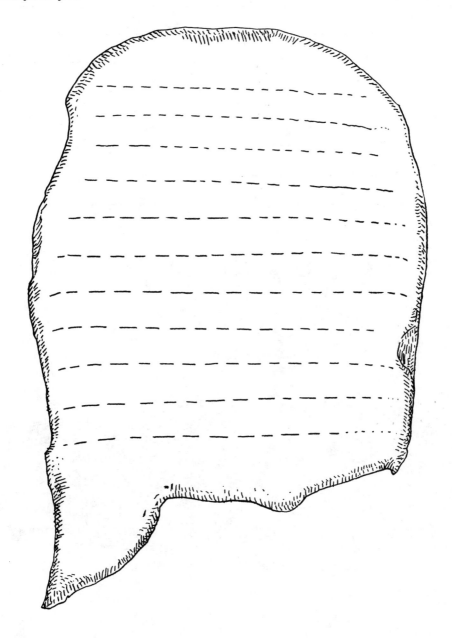

In My Opinion

On page 45 of your textbook you see a picture of ancient Israelites harvesting wheat. The caption tells us that gleaning was an early kind of *tzedakah*. What was gleaning and why was it important?

_____

_____

_____

_____

_____

_____

_____

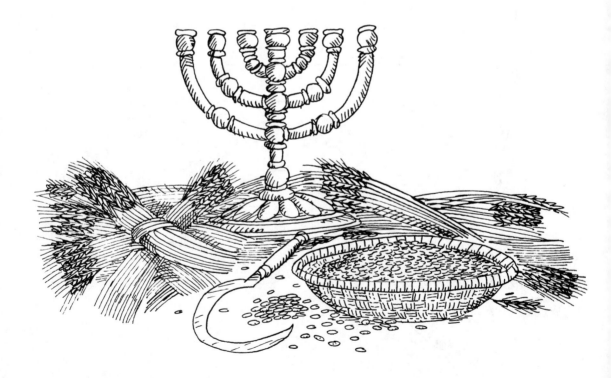

Name Search*

Look across and down to find eleven place names from the days of the two kingdoms. When you find a word, circle it. Write the words you find on the lines below. (Look at the map on page 48 of your textbook if you need help.)

```
P  R  D  A  M  A  S  C  U  S  E

T  V  L  G  I  S  I  D  O  N  T

Y  J  I  F  S  A  M  A  R  I  A

R  U  J  E  R  U  S  A  L  E  M

E  D  N  D  A  M  M  O  N  E  L

T  A  O  O  E  I  L  A  T  D  E

L  H  U  M  L  E  M  O  A  B  T
```

Write the names of the places you found.

_____   _____   _____

_____   _____   _____

_____   _____   _____

_____   _____

Did you find the names of the two kingdoms?

Write them here.

_____   _____

Questions To Answer

1. How did King Solomon gather young men to fight in his army and to build his cities?

_____

_____

_____

2. When the men of the north asked Rehoboam, Solomon's son, not to take their sons, he answered, "My father beat you with whips, but I will whip you with scorpions." What effect did his answer have?

_____

_____

_____

3. For how long did the kingdom of Israel last and how many kings did it have?

_____

_____

_____

4. In those days there were true prophets and false prophets. What role did the true prophets play in Israelite society?

_____

_____

_____

5. What actions of the people most upset the true prophets?

_____

_____

_____

Word Puzzle*

Who was a great true prophet? To find out, fill in the words across. The answer is 1-down.

Across

1. We were slaves there.
2. Where are the ten tribes now?
3. The capital of the kingdom of Israel.
4. He led the Jews into Canaan.
5. We eat matzah on this holiday.
6. The _____ priests offered sacrifices in Jerusalem.

Report The Event

Elijah, and those who were with him, saw a great miracle on Mount Carmel. Write a news article reporting the event for the *Carmel Courier*.

ALL THE MIRACLES THAT ARE FIT TO PRINT.

CARMEL COURIER

WEATHER GOOD DAY FOR A MIRACLE

☆ KINGDOM OF AHAB ☆

Hidden Message*

The prophet Isaiah warned the Judeans. He told the people of Judah that they would suffer the same fate as the people of Israel. Isaiah said:

CEASE TO DO EVIL, LEARN TO
      7   4   5

DO GOOD, DEVOTE YOURSELVES
   10   12   11   3

TO JUSTICE, AND AID THE
1   9   8   2

INJURED.
  6

Write the numbered letters in the circles to see Isaiah's hidden message.

○ ○ ○   ○ ○ ○ ○   ○ ○   ○ ○ ○
1 2 3   4 5 6 7   8 9   10 11 12

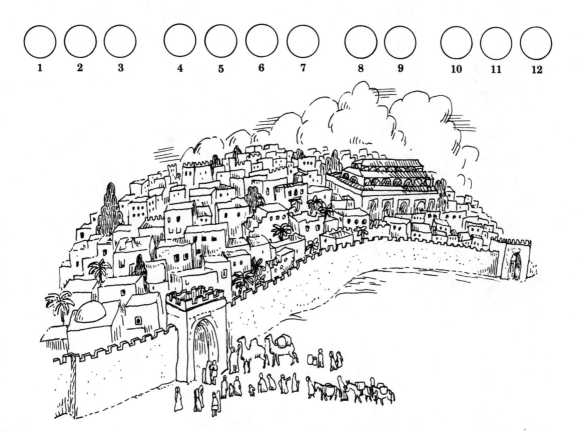

Fill In The Conversations

News of the destruction of the northern kingdom came to Jerusalem. What was the reaction to the news in Judah? Fill in the balloons to show what the people in Jerusalem might have said.

Fill The Box*

Put the first letter of each picture word in the box to find a message of the prophets.

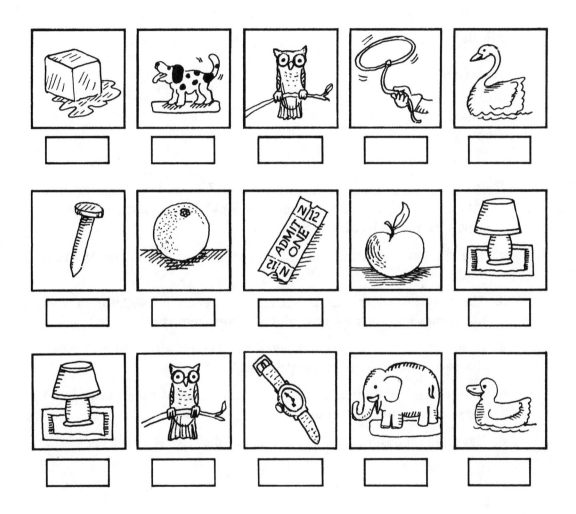

Write the message here:

Who Were They?*

You have read about these people in your textbook. Write each man's name in the sentence that tells about him.

Micah
Ahaz
Hezekiah
Josiah
Sennacherib
Neco

1. King _____ called the people to Jerusalem to hear the holy scroll and asked them to accept the covenant, just as the people had done at Mount Sinai.

2. The prophet _____ warned that Judah was in great danger.

3. The Assyrian ruler _____ encircled Jerusalem with his armies and took away gold and silver from the Temple.

4. King _____ ordered the Temple cleansed and called the people together to celebrate Passover.

5. A weak king of Judah, _____, put up an altar to an Assyrian god in the Temple.

6. Egyptian Pharaoh _____ defeated the king of Judah.

Fill The Box*

Put the first letter of each picture word in the box.

Write the word here.

_____

What happened on this unhappy day?

_____

What Is It?*

These are words from a famous poem.

HOW DO(T)H THE C(I)TY SI(T)
SO(L)ITARY, THAT WAS FULL OF
PEOPLE! HOW IS (S)HE BECO(M)E
AS (A) WID(O)W! SHE TH(A)T WAS
GR(E)AT AMO(N)G THE (N)ATIONS...

Write the circled letters here:

— — — — — — — — — — — —

Unscramble the letters.

The poem is found in the Book of

_____

Be A Scribe

In your textbook, you read that Jeremiah the Prophet dictated his words to his secretary Baruch. Baruch wrote Jeremiah's prophesies in a scroll. It became the Book of Jeremiah in the Bible. There are two quotations from the Book of Jeremiah in your textbook. Choose one of the quotations and write it on the scroll.

How Would You Feel?

First Israel was conquered and then Judah fell. A handful of Jews remained in the land. Most people were sent to Babylonia as captives. For the first time since Joshua conquered Canaan, most Jews lived outside their own land.

Answer one of the two questions below:

How would you feel if you were one of the captive Jews sent to Babylonia?

How would you feel if you were one of the Jews left behind?

_____

_____

_____

_____

_____

_____

_____

_____

Can You Name Them?*

1. He was one of the two prophets who said the time was coming when God would rule the earth.

   _____

2. He said, "The wolf and the lamb shall graze together."

   _____

3. They kept interfering with efforts to rebuild the Temple.

   _____

4. He was an attendant to the king of Persia and he went to Judea to help build the wall around Jerusalem.

   _____

5. He came from Babylonia with holy books to teach the Jews.

   _____

6. He was the Persian king who allowed the people of Judah to return to Jerusalem.

   _____

Report The Event

When Cyrus the Great issued his Edict of Return allowing the Judeans to rebuild Jerusalem, it must have created quite a stir among the Jews of Babylonia. Write a story for the *Persian Press* telling all about it.

EXTRA   **THE PERSIAN PRESS**   USED CAMEL SECTION SEC.3 PAGE 3

BABYLONIA   538 CE

Questions To Answer

1. When Jerusalem was destroyed, most Jews went to Babylonia. Some went to other places. How many places can you name?

_____

_____

_____

_____

_____

_____

2. The Bible speaks poetically of the sadness that overtook the Jews in Babylonia when they thought of their homeland. How did the Jews react?

_____

3. Name a prophet who spoke to the Jews in Babylonia.

_____

4. What is the idea of the prophecy of "The Valley of the Bones"?

_____

5. The Samaritans refused to listen to the laws that the Jews brought back from Babylonia. Can you tell why?

_____

6. The Jews of Babylonia no longer had a Temple. But they made an important discovery. What was it?

_____

Time Line

You are studying Jewish history. The events you have studied in your textbook took place over many centuries. These symbols appear on the inside front cover of your textbook. Write the date over each symbol. Then list one important event that belongs in each time period.

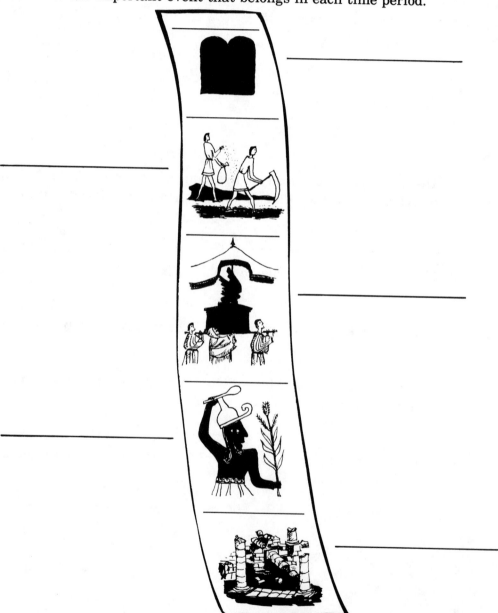

Greek Rebus*

ALEXANDER WAS 🐕 GRR 8.
AT 33 HE D👣ED THE
PERSIANS AND 🐝 CAME
THE 📏[1 2 3 4 5 6 7 8 9 10 11 12] OF THE
🌍. ALEXANDER LET THE
JEWS WOR🚢 AS
T🐐 PLEASED. THE DAYS
DAYS OF THE RABB👁S
🐝 GAN.

_____

_____

_____

_____

Fill The Box*

Put the first letter of each picture word in the box.

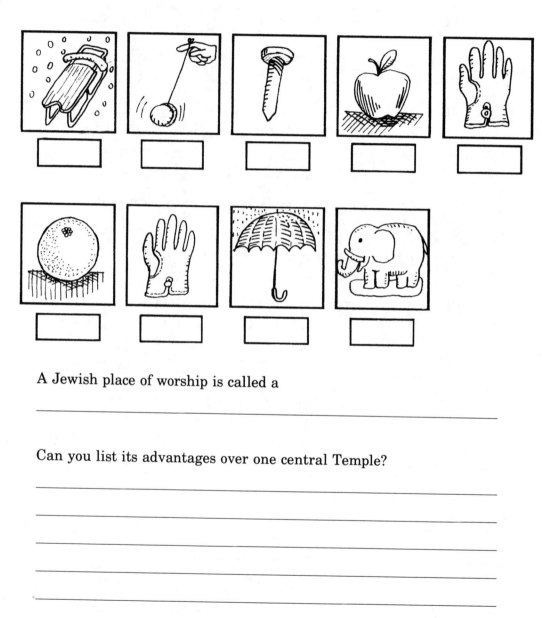

A Jewish place of worship is called a

_____

Can you list its advantages over one central Temple?

_____

_____

_____

_____

Multiple Choice*

Circle the phrase that best completes the sentence.

1. Hellenism means

    a. those who worship Helen of Troy   **b.** the Greek way of life
    c. sports stadiums

2. The Jews of Alexandria spoke

    a. Hebrew   **b.** Egyptian   **c.** Greek

3. The Greek translation of the Torah was called

    a. Souvlaki   **b.** Septuagint   **c.** Arbiss

4. Synagogue is a Greek word meaning

    a. ten men   **b.** house of assembly   **c.** holy place

5. The Greeks practiced

    a. circumcision   **b.** slavery   **c.** the piano

6. The scholars and teachers brought together by Ezra were called

    a. elders   **b.** minyan   **c.** The Great Assembly

7. The number of jewels in the breastplate of the High Priest represented

    a. the wealth of the community   **b.** the twelve tribes   **c.** holiness

8. Many Jews in the Diaspora visited the Temple in Jerusalem on

    a. the three pilgrimage festivals   **b.** Purim   **c.** Yom Ha'atzmaut

9. Religious people who taught that the Greek ways were evil were called

    a. Hellenists   **b.** Hasidim   **c.** mosques

Hasidim vs. Greeks

The Hasidim criticized the Greeks. What were some of the problems they saw caused by Hellenism?

_____

_____

_____

_____

_____

_____

_____

_____

_____

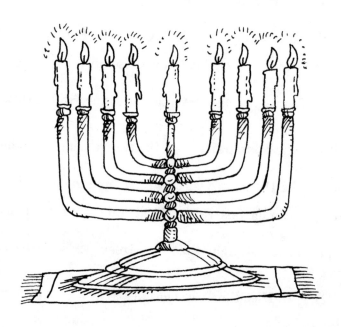

Fill In The Blanks*

You have read that the Syrian ruler wanted the Jews to give up their religious beliefs. Some Jews went along. Most did not. Fill in the blanks to review the situation.

_ _ _ _ _ _ _ _ _ _ tried to get the Jews to adopt Greek

ways. He put a statue of _ _ _ _ in the Temple and began to

sacrifice _ _ _ _ on the altar. As if that were not insult enough,

_ _ _ _ _   _ _ _ _ _ _ _ were torn and burned.

He also banned the _ _ _ _ _ _ _ _. As if that were not

enough, he ordered that anyone found practicing the Jewish

_ _ _ _ _ _ _ _ be put to _ _ _ _ _ _. The Jews took

to the hills in _ _ _ _ B.C.E. and fought back. On the _ _ th day

of the month of _ _ _ _ _ _ they defeated their oppressors.

That is how the festival of _ _ _ _ _ _ _ _ _ began.

Word Puzzle*

What was the family name of Mattathias and his sons? To find out, fill in the words across. The answer is 1-down.

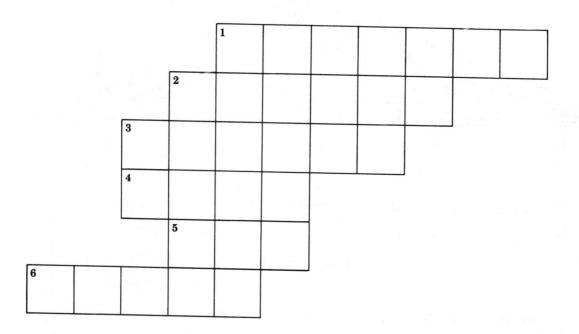

Across

1. The ____ argued against the Hellenists.
2. He spent time in a lions' den.
3. Month in which the Temple was rededicated by the Maccabees.
4. Pompey lived there.
5. Against great odds, the Maccabees did it.
6. He was one of Mattathias' sons.

Design A Banner

Judah, the general after his father Mattathias died, gave his soldiers banners. Draw a picture of the banner they carried. (Be sure to put the Hebrew letters on it.)

Questions To Answer

1. By what popular name was Judah called?

_____

2. What do the Hebrew letters in the name stand for?

_____

3. What does the word mean in English?

_____

4. Why were the Sabbath laws broken?

_____

5. How is the story of Daniel like the story of the Maccabees?

_____

_____

_____

Multiple Choice*

Circle the phrase that best completes each sentence.

1. Apocrypha were books written

   a. by the prophets   **b.** in biblical times but not included in the Bible   **c.** Latin writings

2. The head of the Sadducees was

   a. Ezra   **b.** Shammai   **c.** Zadok

3. The head of the Pharisees was

   a. Hillel   **b.** Ahasuerus   **c.** Daniel

4. Tanach means

   a. Hasmonean king   **b.** Bet Din   **c.** the Holy Scriptures

5. The Pharisees started schools for children in order to

   a. educate everyone   **b.** train soldiers   **c.** keep children busy

6. The —— made the synagogue the center of Judaism.

   a. Babylonians   **b.** Pharisees   **c.** Sadducees

7. The Pharisees taught that Jewish life was based on

   a. a good neighborhood   **b.** the oral and written Torah   **c.** eating corned beef

8. The synagogue grew in popularity when it

   a. also became a house of study   **b.** invited the Romans in   **c.** used an organ

Books Of The Bible

The Bible is divided into three parts. In which part do each of these books belong? Write each book under its correct heading.

Genesis	Amos	Esther
Song of Songs	Joshua	Isaiah
Micah	Leviticus	Daniel
Ezra	Psalms	Exodus
Deuteronomy	Numbers	Ecclesiastes

Torah

_____

_____

_____

_____

_____

Prophets

_____

_____

_____

Writings

_____

_____

_____

_____

_____

Create A Mosaic

The photograph on page 77 of your textbook shows a piece from the floor of an ancient synagogue. The floor is a mosaic. A mosaic is made by putting together many small pieces of colored stone, glass, or tile. You can see another mosaic on page 23. Color in the spaces below to create your own mosaic.

Chain of Tradition

You have read how the Torah was passed from generation to generation. This picture shows the chain of tradition. Fill in the blanks in each link of the chain.

Fill In The Blanks*

In the time of the Second Temple, the _____

_____ met to speak of religious matters. There were

_____ men in this body. Under the Pharisees, a new group arose

called the _____. There were _____ rabbis and

scholars who met in one of the large halls of the _____.

The _____ sat at the head. He was usually from the family of

_____. The _____ sat beside the Nasi. The

rabbis met for two reasons: to discuss matters of _____

and to decide matters of _____.

True Or False*

Circle the letter under True or False.

		True	False
1.	The Hasmoneans made Herod king of the Jews.	A	S
2.	Herod built fortresses and enlarged and expanded the Temple.	A	P
3.	Herod, the great builder, actually came from Idumea.	N	X
4.	All his life Herod feared that one of his buildings would collapse.	E	H
5.	The name of Herod's Jewish wife was Sylvia.	R	E
6.	The Western Wall in Israel is the only remaining part of the wall that surrounded Herod's Temple.	D	P
7.	When Herod died the Jews mourned.	L	R
8.	There were 120 sages in the Great Assembly.	I	O
9.	The Sanhedrin consisted of 71 scholars and rabbis.	N	U

Write the letters you circled in the spaces:
The Supreme Court of the Jewish people was called the

__ __ __ __ __ __ __ __ __.

Map Study

Here is a map outline of Herod's kingdom. Fill in the names on the map to show where

- Herod built a seaport to honor Octavian.
- the Holy Temple stood.
- Herod built a temple to the emperor.
- the river flows between the Dead Sea and the Sea of Galilee.
- there is a city on the shores of the Sea of Galilee.

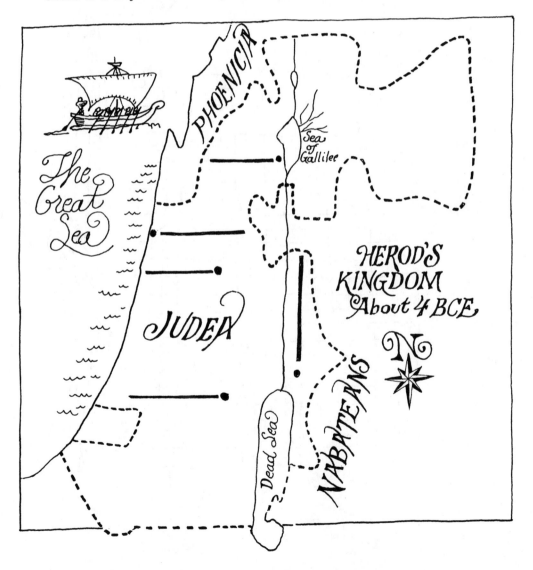

Invisible Word*

Shade in the spaces with dots to see the name of the group that vowed to fight Rome to the death.

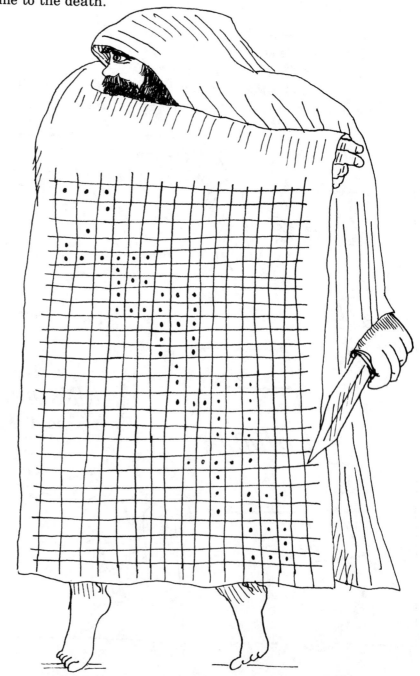

Historical Dictionary

Match the word to its meaning. Write each word next to the correct definition.

aqueduct
crucify
legions
messiah
procurator
publican
Sicarii

a channel that brings water from one place to another _____

Roman soldiers _____

the Jewish savior _____

to kill by hanging on a cross _____

a governor appointed by Rome _____

tax collector _____

zealots who used daggers to kill Romans and Jewish collaborators

_____

Maze

The Jews who survived the destruction of Jerusalem fled to Masada.
From this desert fortress, they fought against the Roman legions. Trace
the Zealots' route from Jerusalem to Masada.

Write Your Own History

You have read that Josephus, commander of the Jewish army of the Galilee, surrendered to the Romans. Josephus wrote a history of the war against Rome. Much of what we know about those times we learn from the writings of Josephus.

Write a page in Josephus' diary, reporting the events that took place at Masada.

_____

_____

_____

_____

_____

_____

_____

_____

_____

_____

_____

_____

_____

Essene Rebus*

THE

SENES LEFT JERUSALEM &

WENT **2** STUD**E** N

THE  **C.** T

COPIED THE HOLY

2 PRESERVE THEM.

W T HEARD T

MAN **4** CES WERE ON

THE THE **S**ENES HID

THE SC  IN CAVES

WHERE THEY LAY **4**

¢**2** RIES.

Who Believed What*

Match the belief to the person or group. Put the number in the circle next to each belief.

1. ZEALOTS
2. PHILO
3. ESSENES
4. PHARISEES
5. PLATO
6. ZOROASTRIANISM
7. STOICS

◯ The Bible is made up of stories about ideas, not about historical people.

◯ Our world is not the true world, for Good rules in the true world.

◯ God would soon send a warrior-messiah.

◯ A final war will take place between the "sons of light" and the "sons of darkness."

◯ The god of light and the god of darkness are always at war.

◯ Jewish life should be centered on the synagogue and study.

◯ Greek myths are not stories about real gods but are tales to teach important lessons.

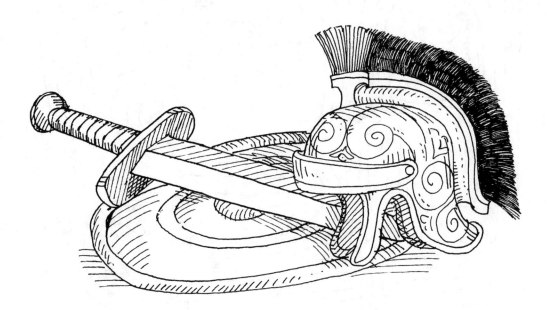

Find The Scrolls

You have read that the Dead Sea Scrolls were found in caves in Qumran near the Dead Sea. Can you find your way through the maze to the scrolls?

Multiple Choice*

Circle the phrase that best completes the sentence.

1. The Temple and Jerusalem were destroyed in the year

    a. 70 B.C.E.   **b.** 70 C.E.   **c.** 7 C.E.

2. Philo was a Greek Jew living in

    a. Greece   **b.** Egypt   **c.** Jerusalem

3. The Jews of Egypt cared far more for _____ than for lost Temple practices.

    a. gymnasium games   **b.** visiting pyramids   **c.** deeds of lovingkindness

4. The Jews of Babylonia were more drawn to _____ than to the rituals of the high priest.

    a. hanging gardens   **b.** philosophy   **b.** synagogues

5. Alexandria, in Egypt, was a

    a. large department store   **b.** city with a large Jewish population   **c.** Roman stronghold

6. The Greek Jews of Egypt said that keeping the law with a good heart was more important than

    a. fasting   **b.** sacrifices   **c.** prayer

7. The Dead Sea Scrolls were

    a. copies of the Bible and other writings hidden by the Essenes
    b. books from a synagogue near the Dead Sea   **c.** Purim scrolls

8. The Book of _____ is missing from the Dead Sea Scrolls.

    a. Daniel   **b.** Deuteronomy   **c.** Esther

Fill The Boxes*

Put the first letter of each picture word in the box.

What is the word?

_____

Why is this place important in Jewish history?

_____

_____

_____

_____

The Work Of The Rabbis*

Who was Hillel's favorite student? To find out, fill in the words across.
The answer is 1-down.

Across
1. Place where a school was founded.
2. Hillel said his student would be the father of —————————.
3. When the student went to teach, he found this one good disciple.
4. Explanations through story and legend.
5. The Aramaic word for teacher.
6. Roman general who became emperor.
7. Supreme court for the Jews.

Questions To Answer

1. Why did Yohanan ben Zakkai disagree with the Temple priests?

_____

_____

2. When Jerusalem was surrounded by the Roman armies, how did Yohanan escape?

_____

_____

3. What did Yohanan request from the Roman Emperor Vespasian?

_____

_____

4. After the Temple was destroyed, Yohanan told his followers that there was another way to ask God to forgive our sins. What was it?

_____

_____

5. What things do we take for granted in Jewish life today that were begun or set down by the Sanhedrin at Yavneh?

_____

_____

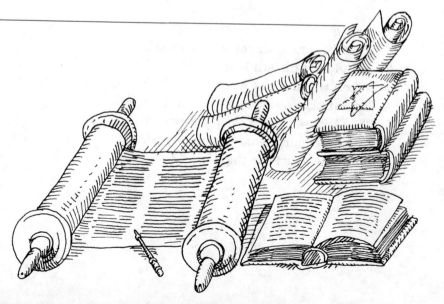

Design A Coin

Coins are like pages in a history book. Often coins commemorate (help us remember) important moments in history. On page 104 in your textbook, you see a picture of an ancient Roman coin. It memorializes Rome's victory over Judea. There are other coins pictured on pages 86 and 90.

Design a coin to memorialize the Sanhedrin at Yavneh.

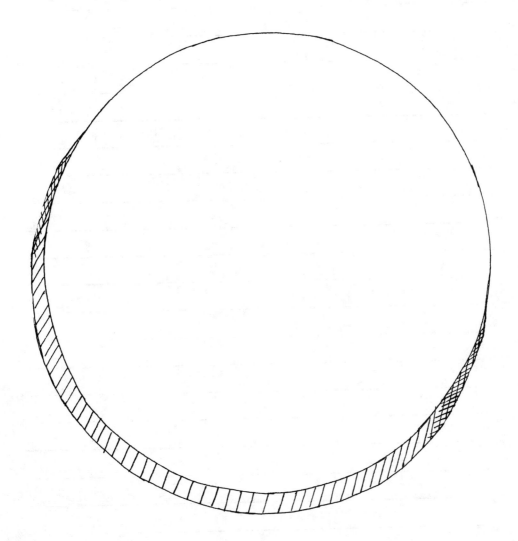

What Is Your Opinion?

In Judea the Jews were fighting a war of national independence. Yohanan ben Zakkai left Jerusalem. Some Jews thought he was a traitor. Yet, in Yavneh, he started a new school and created a new Sanhedrin.
What do you think about Yohanan ben Zakkai's actions?

_____

_____

_____

_____

_____

_____

_____

_____

_____

_____

_____

_____

_____

_____

_____

_____

Invisible Word*

He was a Jewish warrior. Fill in the spaces with dots to see his name.

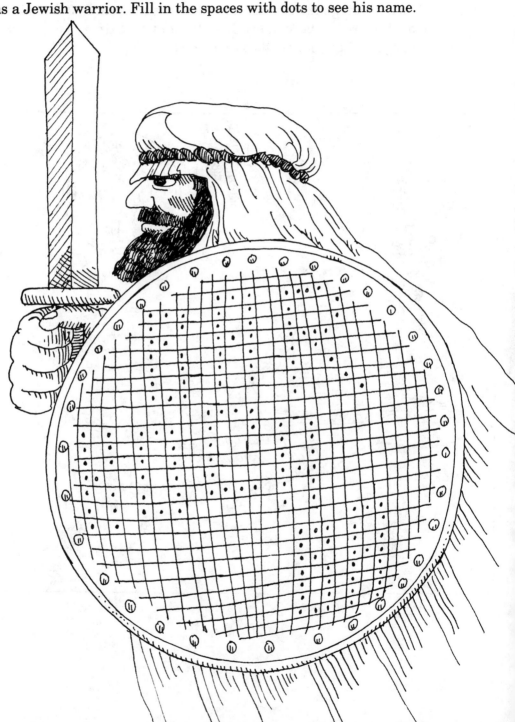

Map Study

This map shows the Roman Empire about the year 300 C.E. Circle and label the areas where many Jews lived at that time. (Look at the map on page 106 in your textbook for help.)

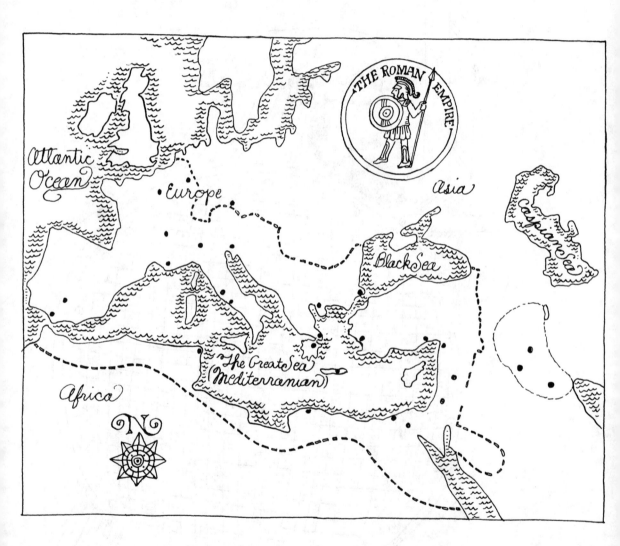

True Or False*

Circle the letter under True or False.

		True	False
1.	The last revolt against Rome began in 132.	R	B
2.	The real name of the Jewish leader was George bar Coziba.	D	A
3.	Rabbi Akiba renamed the warrior Bar Kochba.	B	E
4.	Bar Kochba means "Son of a Star."	B	A
5.	Rabbi Akiba agreed with Yohanan that there were to be no more messiahs.	G	I
6.	The Jewish wars against Rome went on for many years.	A	M
7.	The Romans changed the name of Judea to Palestine to erase the connection between the Jews and their land.	K	L
8.	The Romans renamed the city they had built on the ruins of Jerusalem Aloha Capitolomania.	P	I
9.	No Jew was allowed to enter the city.	B	A
10.	In 135, following the war they had lost, the Jews became a minority in their own land.	A	L

Write the letters you circled in the spaces:

___ ___ ___ ___ ___   ___ ___ ___ ___ ___was a great student of the Torah.

Report The Event

Bar Kochba's revolt failed. The editor of *Caesar's Bugle*, a Roman daily newspaper, has asked you to report this tragic event. Write an article telling what happened from a Jewish point of view.

EXTRA **CAESAR'S BUGLE** THE LATEST GLADIATOR RESULTS

ROME   135 CE

Design A Stamp

The rebellion against Rome in 132 was one of the bloodiest wars the Jewish people ever fought. Design a stamp to memorialize the people and the events.

Fill The Boxes*

The teachings of the Torah are passed from generation to generation. Akiba collected the laws, Meir continued the work, and Judah ha-Nasi finished it.

Put the first letter of each picture word in the box below it to see the name of the book Judah ha-Nasi assembled.

In English the word means

_____.

The six volumes (Orders) of the book are:

_____   _____

_____   _____

_____   _____

The Order dealing with business and criminal laws is called

_____.

Each Order is divided into

_____.

Map Study

Look closely at the map on page 115 of your textbook.

List crops grown in the Land of Israel in the 1st century C.E.	List livestock raised in the Land of Israel in the 1st century C.E.

Define The Names*

Match the name on the left with the correct definition on the right. Write the number next to each name.

Names

HADRIAN _____

AKIBA _____

USHA _____

NASI _____

MEIR _____

BERURIAH _____

SIMON _____

JUDAH _____

PATRIARCH _____

TANNAIM _____

TZADDIK _____

Definitions

1. Home of the Sanhedrin after Yavneh

2. Continued Akiba's work

3. Roman Emperor

4. Roman name for head of the Sanhedrin

5. Rabbi jailed for teaching Torah

6. "Prince"

7. Saint

8. Son of Gamaliel made head of Sanhedrin

9. Great woman scholar

10. Rabbi known as "the Prince"

11. Teachers

My Favorite Teaching

Two thousand years ago, the sages of Israel made important statements about life. Their sayings are found in *Pirke Avot*. Read the Rabbis' teachings on pages 116 and 117 in your textbook. Choose the one you like best and write it here. Then draw a picture to illustrate the lesson.

_____

_____

_____

_____

_____

Babylonian Rebus*

SAM**UL** SAID **2** THE

 SHAPUR," LET

MPLE PRACTICE

T RELIGION.

_____

_____

_____

Hidden Message Puzzle*

What did Rav and Samuel say was better than warfare? To find out, fill in the words across. The answer is 1-down.

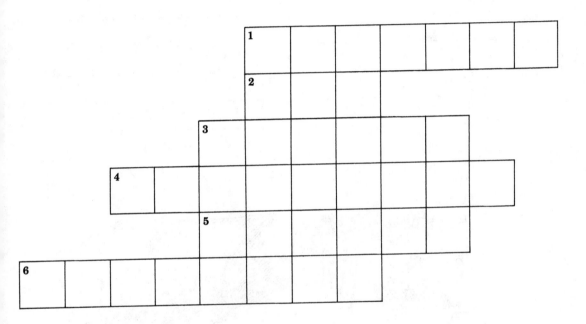

Across

1. Cyrus the Great was one.
2. Teacher who built a school in Sura.
3. Teacher who taught at a school in Nehardea.
4. People who first brought the Jews to Babylonia.
5. Where daily sacrifices had been offered.
6. "Head of the Exiles."

Jewish Occupations

For eight hundred years the Jews of Babylonia lived in peace and freedom. They worked in many different trades. How many Jewish occupations can you list?

_____   _____

_____   _____

_____   _____

_____   _____

_____   _____

_____   _____

Multiple Choice*

Underline the phrase that best completes the sentence.

1. In Babylon, the Jews chose as head of the community a man who
   a. could speak Babylonian   **b.** was from the line of King David   **c.** was rich and famous

2. His title in Aramaic was
   a. Resh Galuta   **b.** Adoni   **c.** Rab

3. Exilarch means
   a. one who is exiled   **b.** President   **c.** Head of the Exiles

4. Jews followed many professions in Babylon, among them
   a. actor   **b.** trader   **c.** astronaut

5. The religion of the Sassanians was called
   a. Parthianism   **b.** Zoroastrianism   **c.** Seleucid

6. Samuel taught Torah and Talmud at
   a. Nehardea   **b.** Harvard   **c.** Naharia

7. Rav taught at
   a. Susa   **b.** Sura   **c.** Babylon University

8. For a long time Babylonia was the greatest
   a. center of Jewish learning   **b.** wine exporter   **c.** seaport

9. The Jews paid taxes and were loyal citizens of Babylonia, and in exchange they were
   a. able to eat with the king   **b.** awarded medals   **c.** free to live as Jews

10. In Babylonia, women were
    a. not permitted to marry until the age of 18   **b.** successful weavers   **c.** in charge of educating the children

Fill In The Word*

1. As Mishnah means _____, Gemara means "what has been learned."

2. Both works together form the _____.

3. While one Talmud was being assembled in Palestine, a second Talmud was being assembled in _____.

4. The _____ Talmud was the larger of the two.

5. All the rabbis whose works were recorded in both Talmuds are called the _____.

6. In English, the word means _____.

7. The Mishnah consisted largely of the laws of Judaism, known as

   _____.

8. Included with the laws were legends and ethical teachings called

   _____.

9. Those who continued to add to the Talmud were called the

   _____.

10. In English, the word means _____.

Time Line

You have studied about many centuries of Jewish history. These symbols appear on the inside back cover of your book. Write the date under each symbol. Then list one important event that belongs in each time period.

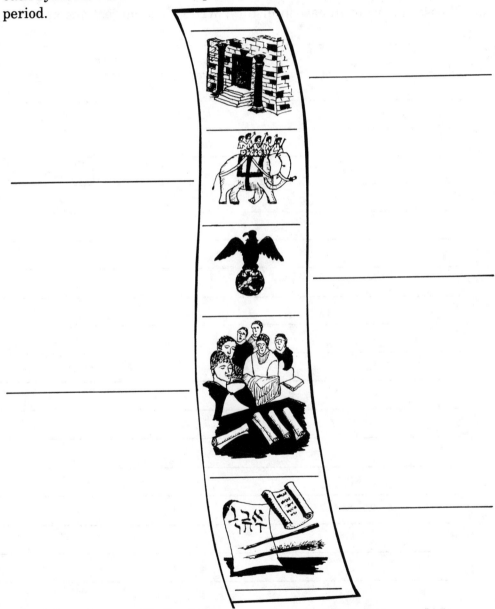

An Event In Jewish History

You have studied about 3,000 years of Jewish history. That's a very long period of time. There may have been some things that surprised you, and some things that impressed you and made you feel proud. Choose one event in Jewish history. Write your impressions here.

_____

_____

_____

_____

_____

_____

_____

_____

_____

_____

_____

_____

_____

_____

Illustrate A Moment in Jewish History

This is the last page in the STUDENT ACTIVITY BOOK. Before long you will continue your journey through Jewish history. Illustrate a moment in our history. Select a person or an event that seems the most important to you. Write an appropriate caption for your picture.

Answer Key*

This activity book has two kinds of questions: those that may be answered by referring to specific facts in the textbook; and those that require the students to interpret the material being studied in the light of their own ideas. The following key provides answers *only* for questions that are factual in nature.

5   *Fill the Box*   MONOTHEISM
7   *True or False*   CANAANITES
9   *Map Study*   BABYLONIA; UR; EUPHRATES; MARI; HARAN; CANAAN; DAMASCUS; SCHECHEM
10   *Adding up History* $12 - 2 + 80 - 83 + 3 = 10$
11   *Find the Hidden Message*   SAFETY; EXODUS
12   *Multiple Choice*   1. b 2. b 3. c 4. a 5. b 6. c 7. c 8. a 9. b 10. c
13   *Word Search*   FORTY; ALTAR; DEW; ARK; CALF; TABLET; SINAI; TORAH; TEARS; MANNA
15   *Word Puzzle*   MANNA (1–down). Across: 1. MOSES 2. WANDER 3. HUNGER 4. HONEY 5. AARON
16   *Find the Hidden Word*   COVENANT
19   *True or False*   MIDIANITES
22   *Fill the Box*   TORAH
23   *Word Puzzle*   JERUSALEM (1–down). Across: 1. JAWBONE 2. SAMUEL 3. ARK 4. SAUL 5. PHILISTINES 6. JONATHAN 7. ALPHABET 8. PURPLE 9. ARAMAIC
24   *Unscramble the Idea*   ONE GOD RULES OVER ALL
25   *Multiple Choice*   1. a 2. a 3. b 4. c 5. a 6. a 7. b 8. a 9. c 10. b
26   *Label the Ships*   GOLD; PRECIOUS STONES; IVORY; SPICES; CEDAR TREES
27   *Find the Hidden Phrase*   ABSALOM WAS KILLED
28   *Multiple Choice*   1. b 2. a 3. b 4. a 5. a 6. c 7. a 8. b 9. c
31   *Name Search*   DAMASCUS; SIDON; SAMARIA; JERUSALEM; AMMON; EILAT; MOAB; TYRE; JUDAH; EDOM; ISRAEL
33   *Word Puzzle*   ELIJAH (1–down). Across. 1. EGYPT 2. LOST 3. SAMARIA 4. JOSHUA 5. PASSOVER 6. HIGH
35   *Hidden Message*   THE LORD IS GOD
37   *Fill the Box*   IDOLS NOT ALLOWED
38   *Who Were They?*   1. JOSIAH 2. MICAH 3. SENNACHERIB 4. HEZEKIAH 5. AHAZ 6. NECO
39   *Fill the Box*   TISHAH B'AV
40   *What Is It?*   LAMENTATIONS

43 *Can You Name Them?* 1. HAGGAI, ZECHARIAH 2. SECOND ISAIAH
3. SAMARITANS 4. NEHEMIAH 5. EZRA 6. CYRUS

47 *Greek Rebus* ALEXANDER WAS GREAT. AT 33, HE DEFEATED THE PERSIANS
AND BECAME RULER OF THE WORLD. ALEXANDER LET THE JEWS WORSHIP AS
THEY PLEASED. THE DAYS OF THE RABBIS BEGAN.

48 *Fill the Box* SYNAGOGUE

49 *Multiple Choice* 1. b 2. c 3. b 4. b 5. b 6. c 7. b 8. a 9. b

51 *Fill in the Blanks* ANTIOCHUS; ZEUS; PIGS; TORAH SCROLLS; SABBATH;
RELIGION; DEATH; 168; 25; KISLEV; HANUKKAH

52 *Word Puzzle* HASMON (1–down). Across: 1. HASIDIM 2. DANIEL 3. KISLEV
4. ROME 5. WON 6. SIMON

55 *Multiple Choice* 1. a 2. b 3. a 4. c 5. a 6. b 7. b 8. a

59 *Fill in the Blanks* GREAT ASSEMBLY; 120; SANHEDRIN; 71; TEMPLE; NASI;
HILLEL; AV BET DIN; RELIGION; LAW

60 *True or False* SANHEDRIN

62 *Invisible Word* ZEALOTS

66 *Essene Rebus* ESSENES LEFT JERUSALEM AND WENT TO STUDY NEAR THE
DEAD SEA. THEY COPIED THE HOLY BOOKS TO PRESERVE THEM. WHEN THEY
HEARD THAT ROMAN FORCES WERE ON THE WAY, THE ESSENES HID THE
SCROLLS IN CAVES WHERE THEY LAY FOR CENTURIES.

67 *Who Believed What?* 2; 5; 1; 3; 6; 4; 7

69 *Multiple Choice* 1. b 2. b 3. c 4. c 5. b 6. b 7. a 8. c

70 *Fill the Boxes* YAVNEH

71 *Name Puzzle* YOHANAN (1–down). Across: 1. YAVNEH 2. WISDOM
3. HANINA 4. MIDRASH 5. TANNA 6. VESPASIAN 7. SANHEDRIN

75 *Invisible Word* BAR KOCHBA

77 *True or False* RABBI AKIBA

80 *Fill the Boxes* MISHNAH

82 *Define the Names* HADRIAN 3; AKIBA 5; USHA 1; NASI 6; MEIR 2; BERURIAH
9; SIMON 8; JUDAH 10; PATRIARCH 4; TANNAIM 11; TZADDIK 7

84 *Babylonian Rebus* SAMUEL SAID TO THE RULER SHAPUR, "LET MY PEOPLE
PRACTICE THEIR RELIGION."

85 *Hidden Message Puzzle* PRAYER (1–down). Across: 1. PERSIAN 2. RAV
3. SAMUEL 4. ASSYRIANS 5. TEMPLE 6. EXILARCH

87 *Multiple Choice* 1. b 2. a 3. c 4. b 5. b 6. a 7. b 8. a 9. c
10. c

88 *Fill in the Word* 1. REPETITION 2. TALMUD 3. BABYLONIA 4. BABYLONIAN
5. AMORAIM 6. INTERPRETERS 7. HALACHAH 8. AGGADAH 9. SABORAIM
10. REASONERS